DUST EATERS

By

JULIE JENSEN

Dramatic Publishing

Woodstock, Illinois • England • Australia • New Zealand

IMPORTANT BILLING AND CREDIT REQUIREMENTS

All producers of the Play *must* give credit to the Author of the Play in all programs distributed in connection with performances of the Play and in all instances in which the title of the Play appears for purposes of advertising, publicizing or otherwise exploiting the Play and/or a production. The name of the Author *must* also appear on a separate line, on which no other name appears, immediately following the title, and *must* appear in size of type not less than 50% the size of the title type. Biographical information on the Author, if included in the playbook, may be used in all programs. *In all programs this notice must appear:*

* * * *

DEVELOPMENT HISTORY

This play's first draft was given a week-long workshop at Salt Lake Acting Company in March of 2003, supported by the Pew Charitable Trusts. David Mong directed, Mike Dorrell was dramaturg, and the cast consisted of Kateri Walker, Valerie Kittel and Robert Scott Smith.

A month later the second draft was rehearsed with the same cast for a public reading at Salt Lake Acting Company, again supported by the Pew Charitable Trusts. On that occasion David Mong and Meg Gibson co-directed.

In November 2003, the fourth draft of the play was given a public reading at Playwrights Theatre of New Jersey, directed by Elizabeth Murphy, dramaturged by Peter Hayes, the cast consisting of Tamir, Debra Cerruti, Michael Irvin Pollard and Steve Mones.

Dust Eaters was supported by the National Theatre Artist Residency Program, administered by Theatre Ccommunications Group and funded by the Pew Charitable Trusts. The play premiered at Salt Lake Acting Company in April 2005 with the following artists:

<u>CAST</u>

Scene I: 1870s

Albertine . . . . LAVONNE RAE ANDREWS
Emma. . . . . JOYCE COHEN
Wesley. . . . . MORGAN LUND

Scene II: 1890s

Estima . . . . JOYCE COHEN
Albertine . . . . LAVONNE RAE ANDREWS

Scene III: 1910s

Pratt. . . . . MORGAN LUND
Carlotta . . . . JOYCE COHEN
Albertine . . . . LAVONNE RAE ANDREWS

Scene IV: 1930s

Lydia . . . . JOYCE COHEN
Enoch. . . . . MORGAN LUND
Albertine . . . . LAVONNE RAE ANDREWS

Scene V: 1950s

Maud Moon. . . . . LAVONNE RAE ANDREWS
Bone. . . . . ERNEST DAVID TSOSIE, III
Enoch. . . . . MORGAN LUND
Lydia . . . . JOYCE COHEN

Scene VI: 1970s

Maud Moon. . . . . LAVONNE RAE ANDREWS
Lydia . . . . JOYCE COHEN
Enoch. . . . . MORGAN LUND

Scene VII: 1990s

Maud Moon. . . . . LAVONNE RAE ANDREWS
Bone. . . . . ERNEST DAVID TSOSIE, III

PRODUCTION STAFF

Director. . . . . DAVID MONG
Set Design. . . . . KEVEN MYHRE
Lighting Design. . . . . JEFF STURGIS
Costume Design. . . . . BRENDA VAN DER WEIL
Sound Design . . . . CYNTHIA L. KEHR
Dramaturg . . . . MIKE DORRELL
Production Stage Manager . . . . TANNER BROUGHTON
Executive Producers . . . . ALLEN NEVINS,
NANCY BORGENICHT

ACKNOWLEDGMENTS

The playwright gratefully acknowledges the expertise and generosity of two Native Americans in the preparation of this play: Kateri Walker, Native American actress and political activist, and Dr. Melvin Brewster, archaeologist for the Goshute Tribe.

PLAYWRIGHT'S NOTE

Dust Eaters is the story of seven generations of struggle in the west desert of Utah between the Goshute Indians and white European settlers.

Mormons always believed that they had a special relationship with Native Americans because *The Book of Mormon* was considered a record of their history. Yet in all essential ways, Mormons treated native peoples the same as other Europeans had: they lied to them, impoverished them, stripped them of their land, and finally relegated them to reservations.

Now, however, the Goshute people have accepted an offer to store high-level nuclear waste on their reservation, located some forty miles from the urban center of Salt Lake City. Needless to say, the white European population is upset.

Although I have considerable experience writing about the history of the West (*Two-Headed* and *Across the Wide and Lonesome Prairie*), and although my ancestors were among the earliest white settlers in the Utah territory, I have never written about Native Americans.

Two aspects of my past, however, prepare me to write this play: one is the fact that during the 1930s my father taught school on the Goshute Reservation, and the other is that he was an amateur archeologist. And so as a child, I spent nearly every weekend tracking through the desert looking for remnants of a long-lost culture, imagining where they lived, where they got water, what they did in the winter and where they sheltered in summer, an exercise in imagination that has never lost its power for me.

I am frequently asked if I am uncomfortable writing this story, since I am not Native American. The answer is yes but that fact also propels the work. The answer to the question of who should tell this kind of story is that we all should. If we shy away from such stories because of ethnicity, we risk leaving our history untold and our mistakes unacknowledged. This is an important story, specific in its details, universal in its applicability. I feel proud to have written it.

— Julie Jensen

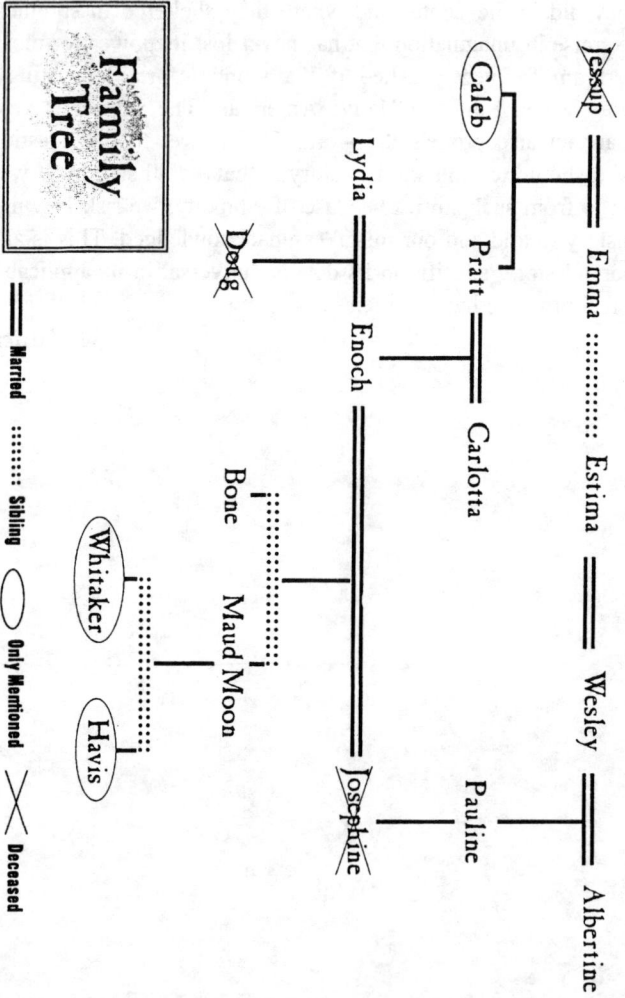

Family Tree

Jessup ═ Emma ·········· Estina ═ Wesley ═ Albertine

Caleb ─ Pratt

Lydia ═ Enoch ═ Carlotta

Doug

Bone

Whitaker ─ Maud Moon ─ Havis

Josephine ─ Pauline

═ Married   ·········· Sibling   ⬭ Only Mentioned   ✕ Deceased

DUST EATERS

A Full-length Play with Intermission
For 2m. and 2w.

CASTING NOTE: This play is intended for four actors:
one Native American woman, one Native American man,
one white woman, one white man. This is not an issue of
doubling, not an issue of economics, it is conceptual.

CHARACTERS

Scene I: 1870s
    WESLEY . . church leader, 50s, grinning, Southern accent
    EMMA . . . . middle-aged woman, slapped but not beaten
    ALBERTINE . . . . Native American girl, 10, feisty

Scene II: 1890s
    ESTIMA. . . . . . . Emma's younger sister, sexy, a bit silly
    ALBERTINE. . . . . Native American woman, 20s, willful

Scene III: 1910s
    PRATT . . . . Emma's son, 45, a rancher, devout
    CARLOTTA. . . wife of Pratt, Scandinavian accent, nervous
    ALBERTINE. . Native American woman, 40s, no one's fool

Scene IV: 1930s
    LYDIA . . . . wife of Enoch, intelligent
    ENOCH . . . Emma's grandson, 30s, a teacher, vulnerable
    ALBERTINE . . Native American woman, 60s, in shock but
    able

INTERMISSION

Scene V: 1950s
  MAUD MOON . . . . Albertine's great-granddaughter, 20s
  BONE. . . . . Maud Moon's brother, 20s, a veteran, fragile
  ENOCH . . . . Emma's grandson, 50s, a farmer, crusty
  LYDIA . . . . Enoch's wife, 50s, eager to make it right

Scene VI: 1970s
  MAUD MOON . . . . Albertine's great-granddaughter, 40s,
    fiery
  LYDIA . . . . Enoch's wife, 70s, fragile, sweet
  ENOCH . . . . Emma's grandson, 70s, ill

Scene VII: 1990s
  MAUD MOON . . . . Albertine's great-granddaughter, 60s
  BONE . . . . her brother, 60s, tribal leader

<u>SETTING</u>

A pioneer house near the Goshute Indian Reservation in the
west desert of Utah. There should be no walls, only a pan-
orama of a sagebrush desert. The table, chairs, a window
and a stove are in all scenes but their treatment changes
through time.

DUST EATERS

Scene I: 1870s

(The lights come up on a large table, set for one, with dishes and cutlery. The surroundings are meager, the feast unusual in this household. A young Native American girl, ALBERTINE, sits in the corner downstage, chanting quietly as she dances a couple of straw dolls around in a circle.)

ALBERTINE *(chanting).*
> *Bioh pahna*
> *Biah vina*
> *Biah vivi oh*
> *Hah nah.*

(EMMA, a middle-aged white woman, rather severe, enters, carrying a large bowl.)

(NOTE: Underscored lines are narration.)

(FURTHER NOTE: In this scene ALBERTINE is only selectively heard.)

EMMA. Take those dolls outside, Albertine. Your attention's needed here.

(ALBERTINE runs out the door and puts the dolls under her apron then reenters.)

<u>This is my Indian daughter, Albertine. She's ten or thereabouts.</u>

(WESLEY enters, a middle-aged white man, a Church leader, with an arrogant grin, and a Southern accent. He sits down and stuffs a napkin in his shirt.)

<u>This is Wesley, my sister's husband. "Come to call."</u>

(EMMA places a large bowl in front of WESLEY.)

<u>And this is my house, such as it is. Built two years ago in 1875.</u>

(EMMA sits at the opposite end of the table without plate or silverware. Long pause as EMMA and WESLEY eye one another. WESLEY grinning.)

WESLEY. I suppose a woman that eats nothing is nourished amply by the pleasure of her guests.

EMMA. Spare me your floral flourishes, Wesley.

WESLEY *(chuckling)*. Without such flourishes, as you call them, how should I compliment your stew?

EMMA. With your silence, Wesley. With your silence.

WESLEY *(chuckling)*. Emma dear, you know me better than that. While I can promise many things, silence is not one of them. *(WESLEY scoots his chair up to the table and looks in the pot.)* Well, well, well. Is this a chicken I see before me?

EMMA. That it is.

WESLEY. Chickens from the southern reaches of this valley, they are more succulent than those from other climes. And I, of course, have been abroad.

EMMA. A chicken is a chicken...is a chicken, Wesley.

WESLEY. These breezes here, from off the salted desert, they enhance the appetite. Brother Brigham says it's true.

EMMA. And so it's true if Brother Brigham says it is.

WESLEY *(smiles at her patronizingly)*. Brother Brigham has eaten from this table, I believe.

EMMA. Brother Brigham has hauled his double-breasted load before this table on more than one occasion. Yes. His urgent business with my husband made him welcome. Always welcome.

WESLEY. And so, dear Emma, he sends his blessings to you now and to your children for whom he asks the special favors of the Lord.

EMMA. I could better use the substance of his larder than blessings from the Lord.

WESLEY. And yet we cannot live without His blessings. Let us bow our heads in supplication to the Lord.

EMMA. In *silent* supplication, if you please.

WESLEY. Whatever you choose.

EMMA. Your attention, Albertine.

(ALBERTINE gets up from the floor, stands behind the table, folds her arms. All bow their heads. A beat. ALBERTINE looks back up.)

ALBERTINE. My *taipo* mother and I ate bones this morning. To keep the hunger away. Now we both must watch

Old Chicken Hawk eat his fill. But I am Lizard in a shadow. I can catch a fly midair. *(She reaches quickly into the pot, takes some meat, and eats it.)*

WESLEY. And so we do and say all this in the name of Jesus Christ, Amen.

EMMA. Amen. Albertine, serve up the stew.

(ALBERTINE obeys.)

WESLEY. Well, well, what a fine young lady. She's even quite pretty.

EMMA. This is Albertine.

ALBERTINE. I am Crow. I fly. I have sharp feet. *(She runs behind WESLEY's chair and claws the air.)*

WESLEY. Her name again?

EMMA. The name is Albertine.

WESLEY. What a pretty name. After the Apostle George Albert Smith, no doubt.

EMMA. Named by my husband when she came to live with us. She has another name. Two or three, in fact.

ALBERTINE. I am *Toya-pin* and *Papuhi.*

WESLEY. And this Albertine, does she perform her duties with a willing heart?

ALBERTINE. If my duty is to stab a stick in you and let the grease run out.

WESLEY. Does she, Sister Emma?

EMMA. Does she what?

WESLEY. Perform her duties with a willing heart?

EMMA. She does.

ALBERTINE. Coyote crouches in her chest. She speaks no truth today.

WESLEY. The future of our Lamenite brethren lies in our hands, you know. We need only consult the scriptures. *Book of Mormon*, Second Nephi, Chapter 30, Verse 6. And I quote, "Many generations shall not pass away among them save they shall be a white and delightsome people."

EMMA. I doubt the literal truth of that.

WESLEY. Seth Murdock claims the girl that stayed with him turned white as a cloud. And it took but seven years.

ALBERTINE *(burping)*. That's for you, Old Chicken Hawk.

EMMA. Albertine, go fetch a glass of milk.

(ALBERTINE sits back on the floor.)

WESLEY. And where's the rest of your little brood, Sister Emma? Caleb and that little pup, what's his name?

EMMA. Parley Pratt.

ALBERTINE. My *taipo* brother. Parley Pratt.

WESLEY. Yes, Parley Pratt. Where are those strapping boys, Emma dear?

EMMA. Exhausted, Wesley...dear.

WESLEY. From the toil of planting?

EMMA. From four days drive to claim the body of their father.

WESLEY. He was an admirable man. Your husband Jessup.

EMMA. An obedient man.

WESLEY. In many ways.

EMMA. Obedient to the point of sheer insanity. He was gravely ill when he left home. His lungs corrupted through and through. We begged the church authorities to excuse him from this call.

WESLEY. And yet he'll reap the richest gifts of heaven. No reward as great as that reserved for those who die in service to the Lord.

EMMA. An empty promise at this point.

WESLEY. Well, it is done, dear Emma, and it is well it is well done.

EMMA. It is not done, Wesley. And it is not well done. I have no means of support.

WESLEY. And it is for that very reason, Emma dear, I've come to call. *(Proudly.)* I've been in conference with the General Authorities.

EMMA. Have you now?

WESLEY. I have indeed.

(ALBERTINE is dancing her dolls.)

ALBERTINE. Mother Deer and Baby Fawn are out in the grass together. Mother Deer puts Baby Fawn down in the grass to rest. "Stay there," she says. "And do not move a hair. Not even if Old Chicken Hawk comes this way." Then Mother Deer moves off behind the tree. *(She hides one of the dolls behind her leg.)* And then Old Chicken Hawk comes stepping through the grass. Step, step. Step, step. Baby Fawn is quiet, doesn't move a hair. Mother Deer is watching Baby Fawn.

WESLEY. And so I am prepared, Emma dear, to make a generous offer.

EMMA. Is that so?

WESLEY. I am prepared to offer you a place within my household.

EMMA. Within your household?

WESLEY. There's nothing I would not do for you, Emma dear.

EMMA. Can that be true, Wesley...dear?

WESLEY. My body aches for you. Has always ached for you.

EMMA. Does it, indeed?

WESLEY. It does. Indeed.

EMMA. Why have you never said as much?

WESLEY. My loyalty to Jessup, respect for the bonds of holy matrimony.

EMMA. Ah, but now?

WESLEY. But now I can express myself more freely.

EMMA. As can I...

WESLEY. But of course that's true.

EMMA. I have not a whit of interest in your matrimonial bed nor membership in a sisterhood of wives.

WESLEY. I see.

EMMA. A sister in my younger sister's home? My sister Estima and I have long been rivals.

WESLEY. And so you'd learn to compromise and get along. As God intended sister wives should do.

EMMA. And what about the land?

WESLEY. This land, this modest little strip of land, would be added to the rest of mine.

EMMA. You buy a ranch for nothing, then? A preposterous proposition—

WESLEY. Excuse me, please. But could I trouble Albertine for yet another serving of your lovely stew? *(EMMA nods at ALBERTINE who serves the stew. They watch her.)* And take that glass and fill it, if you would. *(ALBERTINE puts the glass in front of EMMA.)* You bargain like a trader in the flesh of horses, Emma dear. But I must warn you, nothing raises my blood or admiration more.

EMMA. I can drive a bargain, yes.

ALBERTINE. And I am Lizard. I can move and not be seen. *(She moves behind WESLEY and sticks her tongue out like a lizard.)*

WESLEY. May I assume you'd like to sell the land?

EMMA. I could be persuaded, yes.

WESLEY. Though its size is trifling. The soil poor.

EMMA. Enhanced, however, by a natural spring.

WESLEY. The crops are only modest in their yield.

EMMA. Located conveniently, however. Adjacent to that piece of yours.

WESLEY. And yet it's bordered on the south by Goshute land.

EMMA. A testament to what?

WESLEY. Testament to its basic lack of substance. Goshutes subsist on dust alone.

EMMA. Excellent neighbors, however, for the likes of you. You'll have your way with them.

WESLEY. It's haunted land. Good for nothing more than waiting. A vacant valley waiting. And yet because I care for you, I am prepared to offer, say, thirty head of cattle.

EMMA. What am I to do with thirty head of cattle?

WESLEY. Sell them in the fall, establish you and yours in town.

EMMA. Three times that number. Ninety head of cattle, three to one, beef to dairy.

WESLEY. Out of the question, Emma dear. Let's say forty critters, three to one beef to dairy. That's absolutely all that I can safely do.

EMMA. I have three children, Wesley.

ALBERTINE. I am no child! I am Lizard. I hide with Rock and can't be seen. *(She returns to her corner, crouching.)*

EMMA. I must support them by my own hand.

WESLEY. Though you have two strapping boys to do the heavy labor.

EMMA. They are ten and twelve years old.

WESLEY. And with a fine little herd, of some forty head of cattle, you could begin again. In some new and different land.

EMMA. Though we are established here, remember.

WESLEY. And yet the greatest blessings lie with change. Recall the blessings of the Westward trek.

EMMA. You walked a thousand miles, Wesley, I walked double that. You need not rhapsodize to me about the Westward trek.

WESLEY. At every turn we sought to know the wishes of the Lord, and He was seldom silent if we but bent our heads to listen.

EMMA. And at this time He wants you to deny an aging widow with a brood of little ones?

WESLEY. Very well, I am prepared to make another offer. My final offer.

EMMA. Yes? And what's your offer?

WESLEY. A proposition, really. I'll take the Lamenite girl.

ALBERTINE. I am Baby Fawn. Hiding in the grass. She is watching me. I'm still as wood.

WESLEY. That way, you'll have one less mouth to feed. And Estima another pair of hands.

EMMA. Wesley, no. She's only ten years old. You cannot think you'll marry her. Not yet.

WESLEY. Not yet. But if she proves her worth, she may accomplish that. Now Albertine, there's a girl. Could you serve me up a few more noodles?

ALBERTINE. No. I could not!

EMMA. Serve the noodles, Albertine.

ALBERTINE. Say no to him.

EMMA. Serve up the noodles, Albertine!

ALBERTINE. Not until you tell him no.

EMMA. Obey me, Albertine. At once.

ALBERTINE. I will dump the stew. Watch Old Chicken Hawk lick it from the tabletop.

EMMA. Obey me, Albertine!

(ALBERTINE picks up the ladle, spits in it, then serves the noodles.)

WESLEY. She has a responsive attitude, I see.

ALBERTINE. You do not see. You do not see me. I am crouching Porcupine.

WESLEY *(reaching for ALBERTINE, holding her around the waist)*. You know, young Albertine, the mountain tribes east of here, the Utes, Chief Wakara's people, they took women and children of the desert. Little girls like you. Sold them to the Spaniards. In exchange for horses and for guns. Sold them to the gold-toothed Spaniards. Sold them into slavery. That could have been your fate. Had not the Saints arrived to save the day.

ALBERTINE. For me the Mormons gave two horses and a gun. They took my brother too. And then they took our summer spring, the one with watercress and grass as tall as me.

WESLEY. And you, the lucky little Albertine, a solid roof above your head, a wooden floor beneath your feet. You are most fortunate, indeed.

ALBERTINE. I am Coyote in a cage.

WESLEY. But now, most favorable of all. In these, the latter days, you can learn the story of your people. Not the stories that your dusty race invents, but your true and honest history as recorded in the scripture.

ALBERTINE. Little white lies. Big white liar.

WESLEY. As *The Book of Mormon* says, "...after they had dwindled into unbelief they became a dark and loathsome, and a filthy people, full of idleness and all manner of abomination." That fate awaits you, Little Albertine, unless you learn to read, learn to speak the language.

ALBERTINE. I speak the language of Deer and Bear. I read the sky.

WESLEY. And so I'll take you home with me.

EMMA. Wesley, please, I do not traffic in the flesh of human beings.

WESLEY. Nor do I, my dear. I merely make this offer to relieve you of a burden and to provide a better future for the girl.

EMMA. But I care for her.

WESLEY. And so you'll see her. As often as you like. She's but few miles north of here.

EMMA. I cannot part with her.

WESLEY. Not even for her betterment and yours?

EMMA. She is my helpmate and my solace.

ALBERTINE. I fetch the water from the spring.

WESLEY. Very well, I'll offer in addition the labor of my eldest son for plowing, planting, and bringing in your crops.

EMMA. The labor of your eldest son?

WESLEY. To augment the labor of your boys.

ALBERTINE. Baby Fawn is still as wood.

EMMA. I am little more than a beggar without shoes. I do not see a way beyond the end of summer.

WESLEY. I can take the girl and relieve your economic plight.

EMMA (searches ALBERTINE's face. Quietly:). Very well then, take the girl.

ALBERTINE. So Baby Fawn was caught and killed. And fed to Chicken Hawk.

EMMA. And now I want you out of here. Out of my house and off my land.

WESLEY. Come, Albertine.

ALBERTINE. And Mother Deer heard him say out loud, "How tasty is the flesh of fawns."

WESLEY. Come with me, young Albertine.

(He takes her arm. She wrenches free. ALBERTINE runs back to EMMA. Eyes her with contempt.)

ALBERTINE. Give this ohmaa to Parley Pratt. My taipo brother Parley Pratt. And tell him the Mother Deer has watched Old Chicken Hawk eat her Baby Fawn.

(She hands EMMA the straw doll. EMMA takes ALBERTINE's hand, puts it to her face. ALBERTINE slaps her and pulls away. WESLEY takes ALBERTINE again. She wrenches free again. She goes ahead of him.)

Scene II: 1890s

(Lights up on the same room, more comfortable than in the earlier scene, though still not gracious. ALBERTINE enters, carrying a tablecloth and napkins.)

ALBERTINE. It's a generation later. The 1890s. I'm in my twenties.

(In scoots ESTIMA, energetic, in a nervous tizzy.)

ESTIMA. Give me a hand, Albertine. We've got work to do today.

ALBERTINE. This is Estima, Emma's sister. First wife to Wesley.

ESTIMA. This house is... Well, let's just say, Emma was not the housekeeper I am. And yet it's a blessing we have this little place, to keep us from intrusive eyes. The authorities are watching us, you know. *(She takes the tablecloth and spreads it over a chair.)* But that was a lovely service. Emma would have been well pleased. She was a respected woman, you know, despite her dire poverty.

ALBERTINE. She pays attention to me only when it suits her.

(ESTIMA takes the napkins from ALBERTINE.)

ESTIMA. Now then, Albertine, we must sort out the question of your future. Wesley will be here by noon, and I want it all decided by the time he comes. Of course it's been a rich experience having you a part of our household. We're deeply grateful for the challenge and the reward it's been. For we are a family who has always practiced what the Prophet Brigham Young commanded, as regards your people, "Feed em, don't fight em." And that has meant our peaceful coexistence. But now you must understand that the laws have changed regarding marriage. Are you paying attention, Albertine? *(She exits to get plates and silverware.)*

ALBERTINE. Old Woman and Granddaughter went out to gather pine pitch. Cannibal Giant found them there. He chased them round and round the trees. Old Woman and Granddaughter thought it was a game. Until Cannibal Giant caught them both. And killed them both.

ESTIMA *(reentering.)* What this means is this: only one of us is recognized. Only one of us is legal. That's the law, the newly instituted law. Do you understand this, Albertine?

ALBERTINE. Cannibal Giant ate their flesh. Old Woman and Granddaughter. He ate them both. Except their breasts. Which he hung up in a tree to dry.

ESTIMA. What is it you are mumbling about?

ALBERTINE. Cannibal Giant ate their flesh. Old Woman and Granddaughter. He ate them both. Except their breasts. Which he hung up in a tree to dry.

ESTIMA *(nervous giggle as she folds a napkin)*. And so, Albertine, the law of plural marriage is no longer in effect. And as the first wife, I am, henceforth, the only legal wife.

ALBERTINE *(to ESTIMA)*. Although your brother stayed with his second wife when he got out of prison.

(ESTIMA hears this line, then shakes it off.)

ESTIMA. Now then, we'll finish raising Pauline for you. But the marriage, yours and Wesley's, since it was his fourth, cannot be recognized. Do you understand this, Albertine? Have you anything to say?

ALBERTINE *(out)*. He never touched my breasts. I would not allow it.

ESTIMA. Very well then, could you help me with the table? I want to add a leaf. He could be here any minute. *(Singing.)* "There is sunshine in my soul today, more glorious and bright..." *(They pull apart the table, insert the leaf, and ALBERTINE shoves it closed with her hip. ESTIMA notes it and moves on. Finishing song.)* "...For Jesus is my light!" And we will use my Irish linen for the meal today. Wesley will appreciate that, I think. In prison, of course, there's never a tablecloth at all, let alone a cloth that's crisp and clean. Oh and that's another thing. Now that Wesley's home, the authorities will be watching him. There must be no question of his cohabiting with plural wives. He could be sent to prison yet again for that.

ALBERTINE *(out)*. His breath is sour. His fingers rough. I do not miss Old Chicken Hawk.

ESTIMA. As for Wesley's...*needs*, such as they are in a man of his age, they can be adequately met by me. *(Slight giggle.)* Now then, when you set the table, don't forget to give me the napkin with the hole in it. *(Pause. ALBERTINE says nothing.)* It would help us all immeasurably, Albertine, if you and yours could learn to speak. Even just a nod would help. Now, let's see, how many plates to set. Three plus Wesley. How many plates is that? Can you remember your addition tables, Albertine?

ALBERTINE *(out)*. Two plus two for you is four, four plus
   four for you is eight, and all of everything for you is not
   enough.

ESTIMA *(reciting with an exaggerated rhythm)*.

   One plus one is two.
   Two plus one is three.
   Three plus one is four.
   There's the one we're searching for.
   Hiding there behind the door.
   And yes it is the number four!

There will be four at table today. Set the table for four.
Unless you yourself would like to join us at the end.
Have a piece of pie with us. In which case, that would
be how many? *(ALBERTINE remains silent.)* Five! That
would be five. Set four big plates and a little one. *(AL-
BERTINE does not move.)* You're not working, Albertine. Your mind is casting nets upon the lake?

ALBERTINE. I must brush the dirt on my *taipo* mother's
   grave.

ESTIMA. Of course, you must. We all must work each and
   every day. By the sweat of our brows we shall earn our
   keep. *(Pause.)* But Albertine, you're doing nothing. Are
   you still confused? *(Over articulating.)* The first wife is
   the only legal wife. Other wives are members of the
   family, yes, but not in any way legitimate. Is that clear
   to you?

ALBERTINE *(out)*. I am married when I say I am. Unmar-
   ried when I say I am.

ESTIMA. This does not, of course, resemble the customs
   of your people who marry and unmarry by merely saying so.

ALBERTINE *(to ESTIMA)*. And you marry and unmarry by letting others tell you so.

ESTIMA. Don't be impertinent, Albertine. *(Pause.)* Now then, have you anything more to say? *(ALBERTINE says nothing.)* Of course you haven't anything to say. You people never speak. You must learn to speak.

ALBERTINE. And you must learn to listen.

ESTIMA. If you do not learn to speak, you'll never get ahead.

ALBERTINE. And that is all you want for us.

ESTIMA. But of course, that's what we want for you, your own success.

ALBERTINE. Because you care for us. You cared enough to take our springs and then our land.

ESTIMA. This land is haunted, Albertine. Wesley says it's so. A vacant valley waiting.

ALBERTINE. And so we're fortunate we could give our land to you.

ESTIMA. We want what's best for you. We are a responsible people. *(She indicates a chair for ALBERTINE to sit. And she takes a chair on the other side of the table.)* Now then, I've given your future careful thought. It's clear you cannot return to Indian ways. Your people are all pagan, they're primitive, full of superstition. Whereas you've been raised as white in the fullness of the gospel. You've become accustomed to the better way. With that in mind, I'm pleased to offer you a place within our household. You may stay on here in our employ. You'll have your regular duties. *(Counting them on her fingers.)* Hauling water, doing the wash, the ironing, scrubbing the floors, assisting me in the kitchen, in the garden and with preserving food. All of which you've been

carefully taught to do. In addition, you'll be charged
with care and milking of the cows, care and feeding of
the pigs, including slaughter, as well as care and killing
of the chickens. And this is the best part—I've saved it
for the last—you may sell what's left of the eggs for
your own profit! *(Pause as she waits for a response.)*
"Thank you, ma'am"? "Please" and "thank you,"
Albertine. Do not forget your manners.

ALBERTINE. I can be your farm worker. I can be your
house servant.

ESTIMA. It represents an increase in responsibility. But I
think you're up to the challenge.

ALBERTINE. I am so grateful…

ESTIMA. Good, I thought you would be.

ALBERTINE. …to be enslaved by you.

ESTIMA. Your English, Albertine. A worker and a slave
are much, much different. *(Leaping up.)* Now then, you
may stay here on the property, if you wish. There is the
little shed out by the lambing pens. You could get a
stove. Wouldn't that be nice?

ALBERTINE. I do not want a shed.

ESTIMA. You'll need something, Albertine. It can get very
cold in winter.

ALBERTINE *(out)*. Cold as a white man's bargain.

ESTIMA. Now then, there's water nearby. The spring with
watercress. That's near the shed. You can have a little
garden plot. You'll want for nothing.

ALBERTINE *(out)*. Except my freedom.

ESTIMA. I've thought it through and through. I know it's
best for you.

ALBERTINE *(out)*. Four days south of here, in the land of
the Paiutes, Wavoka had a dream.

ESTIMA. The other sister wives will live together in the little house below the spring. They'll raise barley, oats, and dry land wheat.

ALBERTINE *(out)*. There will be an earthquake and a flood. The whites will smother in a landslide. Most of you will die. The rest of you will turn to fishes in the rivers.

ESTIMA. What are you mumbling, Albertine?

ALBERTINE *(to ESTIMA)*. Wavoka had a dream. God spoke to him. If we all unite, all tribes and bands, the dead will wake again.

ESTIMA. Oh, Albertine, you can't believe such things.

ALBERTINE. God speaks to us in dreams.

ESTIMA. We all have dreams. They do not mean a thing.

ALBERTINE. If we join together, all tribes, all bands, and dance as we are told, we'll wake the dead. And Grandmother Earth will be as she was before you whites arrived.

ESTIMA. Hush now, Albertine, that's rude! Need I remind you that you are a member of the Church of Jesus Christ, the only true religion. You know better than to place your trust in the ravings of false prophets.

ALBERTINE. We dance four days, and on the fifth, we dance all night. And then we're ready.

ESTIMA. Ready for exactly what?

ALBERTINE. Ready for the dead to wake.

ESTIMA. The waking of the dead? My gracious, listen to yourself.

ALBERTINE. I sound like you.

ESTIMA. You will not compare my trust in God with the rantings of a savage, a man who finds the truth in dreams.

ALBERTINE. Joseph Smith found truth in *visions*.

(ESTIMA slaps ALBERTINE.)

ESTIMA. Forgive me, Albertine. But you must be taught a lesson. Do not compare the prophet of the Lord with an illiterate Indian that dreamed a dream.

ALBERTINE. Because I trust the teachings of Wavoka, I will not strike you back.

ESTIMA. You must be taught a lesson, Albertine.

(ALBERTINE takes off her apron. Underneath is a Native shirt.)

ALBERTINE. If I wear this shirt, no harm will come to me.

ESTIMA. Oh come now, Albertine. You know better than that.

ALBERTINE. You have a shirt for your protection.

ESTIMA. Those are sacred garments, anointed by the divinely established authority of Jesus Christ.

ALBERTINE. And the Indians that don't believe, who do not dance, they'll turn to wood and burn in fires.

ESTIMA. Burn in fires, Albertine? They're threatening you.

ALBERTINE. The earthquake and the flood will come this spring. The waking happens in the autumn, this coming autumn.

ESTIMA. You know the date, do you?

ALBERTINE. I will see my mother and my father again. I'll see my brother and my sisters. My grandpa and my grandma. There will be a rabbit drive. With all of us together on the earth that's clean for us.

ESTIMA. Albertine, it's time to put away these silly thoughts. Wesley could walk in that door at any moment. *(ALBERTINE begins to apply a brick-red paint to her face. The sound of a drum in the distance.)* And you may not paint your face! You know the rules. You may not bring your war paint in this house.

ALBERTINE. This is sacred paint.

ESTIMA. Stop that at once. Albertine.

(ALBERTINE begins a side-step dance.)

ALBERTINE. We'll go to Wounded Knee. To the land of the Lakota. Dance together, all of us, the seven bands of the Sioux, the Arapaho, the Cheyenne, the Shoshone.

ESTIMA. If you want to go somewhere, go to the reservation with the Utes. As you've been assigned to do. Join the Utes on their allotted lands.

ALBERTINE. When *you* join the English on their allotted lands. Goodbye, Estima.

ESTIMA. And you're *not* leaving.

ALBERTINE. I'll take Pauline with me.

ESTIMA. But I told you I would take her. Raise her here.

ALBERTINE. She's my daughter. She goes with me.

ESTIMA. To be raised in filth and squalor?

ALBERTINE. The animals do not live in squalor. They live like us.

ESTIMA. I will not allow it.

ALBERTINE. She'll be raised by people who will not turn her out. Who will not eat her flesh and hang her breasts on trees.

ESTIMA. She's Wesley's daughter too, don't you forget.
ALBERTINE. She was never more to him than a little spi-
    der on his leg.
ESTIMA. But Albertine...
ALBERTINE. Yes.
ESTIMA. You are forbidden.

*(ALBERTINE, now in her Ghost Dance Shirt and
painted face, stares at ESTIMA and begins a chant.)*

ALBERTINE.
    Oiso Poh
    Oiso Poh
    Tumattikan
    Tumattikan
    Hei!

(Blackout.)

Scene III: 1910s

*(Lights up on the same room. A porch has been added to
the house. CARLOTTA enters, a nervous woman, with a
Scandinavian accent. She carries a tray with the dishes
for the midday meal, which she sets out.)*

CARLOTTA. It's twenty years later, 1918. My husband
Pratt. Hard worker, as you can tell.

(PRATT enters and sits at the table.)

We got his mother Emma's old house. Trying to make a go of the farm, such as it is. Out here in the middle of nowhere. And of course, there's the baby now. Little Enoch. *(She sits. PRATT begins eating. A beat. CARLOTTA watches him nervously. Blurting out:)* Because they blend in with the shadows somehow. Take you by surprise.

PRATT. Don't be ridiculous.

CARLOTTA. Don't want nothing that dirty around me. Nothing that dark.

PRATT. Carlotta, please. Pass the gravy, would you?

CARLOTTA. But they scare me, Pratt. The look of them scares me. The smell of them.

PRATT. There is nothing to be scared of!

CARLOTTA. There most certainly is.

PRATT. No, Carlotta, there isn't.

CARLOTTA. "The scourge of the plains"?

PRATT. Eat something, would you? You're not eating anything.

CARLOTTA. That woman south of here. In the foothills of the Stansbury Mountains. Terrified for the rest of her life. *Died* terrified.

PRATT. That happened thirty years ago, Carlotta. At a time of war.

CARLOTTA. What about those militants against the draft. Goshutes with guns!

PRATT. Controlled by federal troops, Carlotta. Listen here, we are far more dangerous to them than they are to us.

CARLOTTA. That's what people say about snakes.

PRATT. Because it's true. Pass the bread and have done with this. *(She hands him a plate. Pause.)*

CARLOTTA. Dust Eaters. That's their tribal name. Because they eat dirt?

PRATT. A name the Paiutes gave them as a joke. Because they dig up roots. Now enough!

CARLOTTA. Enoch is frightened of them. Little Enoch.

PRATT. He's too young to be frightened of them.

CARLOTTA. He tenses up, seizes up. I can feel his little body. Tensing up. Whenever one is near.

PRATT. He's five months old, Carlotta. Everything he knows, he's learned from you. Look here, why don't you come with me this afternoon. I'll give you a shovel. You can help me put in that dam on the spring. Get your mind off this. *(Pause.)*

CARLOTTA. I think they do it on purpose.

PRATT. Do what?

CARLOTTA. Look that way.

PRATT. Look what way? Pass the butter.

CARLOTTA. They know how to set us off. They do it to set us off.

PRATT. They do nothing of the sort.

CARLOTTA. And why ain't they over on the Ute Reservation? That's where they belong.

PRATT. Goshutes and Utes don't get along.

CARLOTTA. Since when?

PRATT. Since forever.

CARLOTTA. That's the worst thing about you being the bishop. We got them crouching on the porch, hunched in the yard all the time.

PRATT. It ain't all the time.

CARLOTTA. That woman this morning, standing right in front of the window, looking straight in.

PRATT. If you can look out, why can't she look in?

CARLOTTA. Because it is rude!

PRATT. Maybe she thinks it's polite. Mind if I take the rest of these turnips?

CARLOTTA. Then she just come up to the door and knocked like she was...a person.

PRATT. Did she give her name?

CARLOTTA. Of course not. Just stood there looking out from under her hair. *(A knock is heard.)*

PRATT. I'll get it.

CARLOTTA. Pratt... *(He stops. Looks at her.)* If it's them again, you can give them something to eat. But I ain't having them in the house. And I mean what I say, Pratt.

(She leaves the room. He goes to the door. It's ALBER-TINE, now in her 40s, with cropped hair and blood on her face. He looks at her for a moment.)

PRATT. Albertine?

ALBERTINE. What happened to your hair?

PRATT *(chuckles)*. What happened to yours?

ALBERTINE. You think our mother Emma would not approve?

PRATT. I think she would not. *(He studies her.)* You look a little older. But healthy. Are you healthy?

ALBERTINE. Yes. Yes, of course. You've painted the house. Added a...

PRATT. Porch.

ALBERTINE. Porch.

PRATT. My wife's idea.

ALBERTINE. Like standing on a square cloud.

PRATT. I guess so.

ALBERTINE. Well, it'll give you something to sweep.

PRATT. Yes. *(He smiles in recognition.)*

ALBERTINE. I brought you these. *(She hands him a pair of tanned leather gloves; they have large cuffs, beadwork and fringe.)*

PRATT. Beautiful gloves.

ALBERTINE. Buckskin.

PRATT. Someone must have died. *(ALBERTINE nods.)* Fine beadwork. Thank you.

ALBERTINE. Welcome. *(Pause.)*

PRATT. I'd invite you in, but—

ALBERTINE. But your wife can't stand the sight of me.

PRATT. Well, she's a little fussy, you know.

ALBERTINE. Fussy. Not something that happens to us.

PRATT. No, I guess not. I still have your little straw doll. The *ohmaa.*

ALBERTINE. Oh yes, the Mother Deer.

PRATT. And where is Baby Fawn?

ALBERTINE. She was eaten by Old Chicken Hawk, don't you remember? While Mother Deer looked on.

(PRATT nods. Nothing to say.)

PRATT. Magpie feathers in your hair?

ALBERTINE. Yes.

PRATT. Women can have them now?

ALBERTINE. They're my husband's.

PRATT *(with a grin).* Better hide them good, or I might just steal them.

ALBERTINE. And in the middle of the night, too.

PRATT. I stole them, all right. But I had them for less than an hour before I buried them. Out by the stack yard. I was afraid I'd die if I kept them.

ALBERTINE. And so you would have.

PRATT. I know. *(He smiles.)* Where are you now?

ALBERTINE. Standing on your shiny white porch. Looking at your shiny white head.

PRATT. Where are you living?

ALBERTINE. In the stand of cottonwoods down by the spring.

PRATT. No, I mean where are you *living*?

ALBERTINE. In that stand of cottonwoods.

PRATT. But just for the next few days.

ALBERTINE. Until we move on.

PRATT. You're not just a...vagabond.

ALBERTINE. No. I'm free.

PRATT. Not free from want. *(Pause.)* Is Pauline with you?

ALBERTINE. Yes. Married. A child of her own. A girl. Josephine.

PRATT. Josephine. Named after Joseph Smith?

ALBERTINE. No. Named after Chief Joseph.

PRATT. And Pauline. She married an Indian?

ALBERTINE. She *is* an Indian.

PRATT. Well, my Uncle Wesley might disagree with you.

ALBERTINE. All right, she's half. But the better half.

PRATT *(looks at her again)*. You know, you look a sight. My mother would have a fit.

ALBERTINE. So would mine. But my husband died.

PRATT. I'm sorry.

ALBERTINE. Influenza. One of your white man diseases. Those gloves were his.

PRATT. That's why there's blood all over you.

ALBERTINE *(nodding)*. In mourning.

PRATT. Little wonder you frightened my wife.

ALBERTINE. Little wonder.

PRATT. Terrifying, when you think about it.

ALBERTINE. It's not terrifying.

PRATT. Extreme, then.

ALBERTINE. So is death.

PRATT. And your hair?

ALBERTINE. Cut it when he died.

PRATT *(eyeing her)*. You've reverted, haven't you?

ALBERTINE. No, I've returned!

PRATT. You've reverted!

ALBERTINE. You just can't follow me anymore!

PRATT. Listen, I don't want you people going into that pasture down there by the spring. I'm putting a dam in. And I don't want you inside that fence. I got cattle in there, and I don't want you scaring them, tromping through the water.

ALBERTINE. We used to camp down there in the fall. After pine nut season, before the rabbit drive. Wait for the antelope to come through. Long before any of you were here.

PRATT. Indians been in the water, cattle won't drink afterward.

ALBERTINE *(ironically)*. Is that right?

PRATT. That's right. Especially with blood all over you. They smell it. They won't drink.

ALBERTINE. For a smart white man, you hold a lot of superstitions.

PRATT. My father told me that. And I believe it's true.

ALBERTINE. It ain't true, Parley Pratt. But I won't get inside your fence. Won't mess with your dam. *(Awkward pause.)*

PRATT. You need food, I suppose.

ALBERTINE. Since you've scared off the antelope, yes.

PRATT. If you can work, we can feed you.

ALBERTINE. If I can work?

PRATT. New policy from the Church.

ALBERTINE. What happened to "feed em, don't fight em"?

PRATT. This is a new policy. We're instilling the work ethic.

ALBERTINE. 'Course, I was your sister once.

PRATT. That has nothing to do with this.

ALBERTINE. ...Pulled you out of that spring down there, choking and spitting. If it weren't for me, you'd be laying next to Emma now, out in the back yard, under a little mound of dirt!

PRATT. You're an Indian, Albertine. We can't afford to encourage bad habits!

ALBERTINE. Can't afford Christian charity neither, I guess!

PRATT. You're always fighting about something. Always had a chip on your shoulder.

ALBERTINE. Just because I wouldn't do everything you said—

PRATT. Mother could never make you behave.

ALBERTINE. I'm no one's slave!

PRATT. And you can't get along with your own people either. Why ain't you still in South Dakota? And what *were* you people thinking, anyway? Dancing with ghosts.

ALBERTINE. I survived a massacre, Parley Pratt. One of the few. Hid under a sagebrush and pretended to be dead. Later I watched them throw the frozen bodies of the dead Indians in a pit I helped to dig.

PRATT. I'm sorry.

ALBERTINE *(pause. This is difficult for her to say)*. Look, Pratt, there's a dozen of us down at the spring. We ain't eaten in four days.

PRATT. Oh, my God...

CARLOTTA *(calling from offstage)*. Who is it, Pratt?

PRATT. I'll take care of it.

(CARLOTTA comes up to the door.)

CARLOTTA *(whispering)*. My God, she's a sight. Smells like a bonfire, looks like a banshee. Give her some soup, but don't let her in.

PRATT. Let me handle this. Please.

CARLOTTA *(whispering)*. She can't come in here. And make sure she gets the hair out of her eyes.

ALBERTINE. She speaks of me as if I were dead.

CARLOTTA *(whispering)*. If she cleans up, she can eat on the porch. Otherwise, I want her off my lot.

PRATT. I'll take care of this, Carlotta.

(ALBERTINE and CARLOTTA stare at one another. AL-BERTINE jumps. CARLOTTA runs.)

ALBERTINE. She's a wonderful person, Parley Pratt. Generous and brave.

PRATT. She has other qualities.

ALBERTINE. Keeps the house well dusted.

PRATT. In a manner of speaking, yes.

ALBERTINE. Well, that must be nice. Helps you remember who you are. Clean and bright, light and white.

PRATT. Listen, you can have something to eat, but I want you to help Carlotta with the laundry this afternoon.

ALBERTINE. I ain't working in the heat of the day.

PRATT. If there's daylight, you work. That's the rule. That's what it takes.

ALBERTINE. I don't work in the heat. I'm not crazy.

PRATT. You sit around waiting for someone to give you a handout instead.

ALBERTINE. We work till we have enough for that day.

PRATT. And in the meantime, you live in brush houses.

ALBERTINE. And you live in a square prison.

PRATT *(change of tone)*. You gotta help me out here. You gotta clean up. *(Chuckle.)* Don't want you mistaken for an animal.

ALBERTINE. I am an animal, Pratt, and so are you.

PRATT. I think I've risen above that.

ALBERTINE. No, Parley Pratt, you ain't. And one day maybe you'll understand it. One day, if you're lucky.

PRATT. Sit down, right where you are.

ALBERTINE. What for?

PRATT. I'm washing your face. *(He grabs her. She twists away from him. Sits down on her own.)*

ALBERTINE. You can wash my face. But it won't change a thing.

PRATT. It changes a lot. I can't stand to look at you. *(He grabs a rag and a bucket.)*

ALBERTINE. On the day you die, if not before, you will understand.

PRATT. We are a civilized people. Doing our best to civilize the rest of you.

ALBERTINE. On that day you will join the rest of creation. One of many. Distinct in no way at all. A small part of the whole. A very small part.

PRATT. That's enough, Albertine.

ALBERTINE. Where is your civilization then? Your fences, your dams, your ninety head of cattle.

PRATT. And when I'm finished, we'll put you in clean clothes.

ALBERTINE. So that at last I can become both whitesome and delightsome?

PRATT. Hush up and sit still. *(He begins to scrub her face. She stops him.)*

ALBERTINE. Coyote lost her brother, Wolf. She watched the enemy kill him, then skin him. She followed after them, and when it was night, she took back her brother's hide. She kept it wet, and every morning looked to see if her brother Wolf had returned to her. Then one morning she heard her brother howling. So she followed the sound. But it got farther and farther away. The more she traveled, the more distant the sound. Coyote never found her brother. *(PRATT pauses. Hands her the rag.)* Now I will be white enough to clean your floors. *(ALBERTINE washes her face, her eyes glued to PRATT.)*

Scene IV: 1930s

(We're in the same house. There are chintz curtains and a large sideboard. A porcelain figurine sits on the table. It is night. Sounds of a storm outside. LYDIA enters, an intelligent woman. She checks the window.)

LYDIA. It's 1938, a generation later. Enoch and I got married a few years ago. He teaches for the Indian Service. This is his grandmother Emma's house. It's a good solid house, but no electricity yet. *(She hears a sound on the porch. Calling to him.)* Enoch!

(ENOCH enters from the outdoors, wet from the rain, blood all over him. He looks vacant.)

LYDIA. You couldn't save her then?

ENOCH. No.

LYDIA. And she…just bled to death.

ENOCH. She hemorrhaged, yes.

LYDIA. Albertine is here. She brought the baby.

ENOCH. Get me some water, would you?

LYDIA. She thinks she's supposed to clean. I told her it's night. She doesn't work at night.

ENOCH. We gotta clean that schoolroom before tomorrow morning.

LYDIA. That's where you did it? In the schoolroom?

ENOCH *(exploding)*. Where else would you suggest?

LYDIA. Not in her house, I guess. Dirt floor.

ENOCH. Couldn't drive her to the hospital. An hour and a half from the goddamn hospital. Get me some water!

LYDIA. Sorry. *(She gets a pitcher of water. He washes in a bowl.)*

ENOCH. Gotta get out of this godforsaken valley. Vacant, haunted place. Get a job in the civilized world. God-damn drought. Goddamn Depression.

LYDIA. Where is she now—Josephine?

ENOCH. They took her to the dance hall.

LYDIA. I told Albertine to come in here by the stove. But she wanted to work.

ENOCH. Just like cattle. Always give birth on the coldest damn night of the year.

LYDIA. It is not her fault.

ENOCH. Of course it's not Josephine's fault, she's dead. Hand me that towel. *(She does. He wipes his hands.)*

LYDIA. Why do you suppose that is? Giving birth in storms.

ENOCH. Nature's way of culling the weak.

LYDIA. That's so cruel.

ENOCH. Nature's cruel. Look at Josephine.

(ALBERTINE enters, now in her 60s, she's in shock, but still able. She carries a small pile of ENOCH's clothes.)

ALBERTINE. I need to burn the clothes now. *(ALBERTINE opens the fire door on the stove.)*

LYDIA. No, Albertine. We don't burn Enoch's clothes, we wash his clothes. *(She takes the clothes from ALBERTINE.)*

ALBERTINE *(staring at ENOCH)*. I heard the water babies singing.

ENOCH. I heard them too.

ALBERTINE. We all heard the water babies singing.

ENOCH. Yes.

LYDIA *(to ENOCH)*. What's she talking about?

ALBERTINE. That's how we know someone will die.

LYDIA. Oh I don't think so, Albertine. We cannot know these things.

ALBERTINE. You must take the dam out of the spring. The water babies tell us so.

ENOCH. I know how you feel about that dam.

ALBERTINE. You must do it.

ENOCH. I can't, Albertine. I need the water.

ALBERTINE *(still fixed on ENOCH)*. The baby's a girl.

LYDIA. Yes, I know. Do you have a name for her?

ALBERTINE. *Taipo Mea.*

LYDIA. White girl?

ALBERTINE. White Moon.

LYDIA. Well, that's very nice. Would you like to sit down? *(ALBERTINE exits.)* What should I do with her?

ENOCH. Nothing. Let her go.

LYDIA. I think she's crazy.

ENOCH. We're all crazy.

LYDIA. You know she's got that baby, only hours old, strapped to a cradleboard.

ENOCH. That's how they handle them.

LYDIA. She's got it hanging on the wall.

ENOCH. That won't hurt it.

LYDIA. It's the idea of it. That baby's up on our bedroom wall.

ENOCH. So the hell what, Lydia!

(ALBERTINE enters wearing the cradleboard and the baby laced inside. She stands with her back to the stove, warming the baby.)

LYDIA. Let me hold the baby, Albertine.

ALBERTINE. The baby's fine.

LYDIA. But I'd like to hold her. I could wash her off.

ALBERTINE. Baby Moon is fine.

LYDIA. I'm sure she is, but maybe she shouldn't be confined like that.

ALBERTINE. She likes her cradlebasket.

LYDIA. Stunts their growth, you know, lacing them up.

ALBERTINE. This is the way we do it.

LYDIA. Delays muscle development. Small and large motor development. And if babies don't crawl, they're behind, both mentally and physically.

ENOCH. Jesus, Lydia, the baby's an hour old.

LYDIA. And I have a degree in child development! *(ENOCH retreats.)* I'm worried about the baby, Albertine. Who's going to raise her?

ALBERTINE. I will raise her.

LYDIA. But you're the great-grandmother, aren't you?

ALBERTINE. Yes.

LYDIA. That's not a good idea. More and more, they're saying that it's not a good idea. Babies are meant to be raised by their mothers, people their mother's age. It's not a good idea to skip generations.

ENOCH *(muttering)*. If that's the least of her goddamn problems. *(He searches for a match.)*

LYDIA. Besides you're already raising the little boy. The one with the curls. What's his name?

ALBERTINE. Little Bone.

LYDIA. Little Bone, yes. And don't you have your hands full with him?

ENOCH. This does not concern you, Lydia.

LYDIA. I mean, don't you think you've got enough, more than enough with Little Bone?

ENOCH. It's none of our business.

LYDIA. I'm just wondering if you don't feel like an old woman, Albertine.

ALBERTINE. The earth is a grandmother.

LYDIA. I see. Well, that's a lovely thought.

(ALBERTINE exits. ENOCH lights a coal oil lamp, puts it on the table.)

LYDIA. I saved you some dinner if you'd like something to eat.

ENOCH. I'm not hungry. *(Pause. He sits and stares at the flame.)*

LYDIA. Could you have saved Josephine, if they'd come for you earlier?

ENOCH *(shaking his head)*. She was breech.

LYDIA. Can't you turn them?

ENOCH. Not after they drop.

LYDIA. So you had to cut her out?

ENOCH. I asked them first.

LYDIA. Of course.

ENOCH. I said, "Should I cut her out?" They said yes. Well, they didn't say yes. They never say anything. They just nodded. So I did it. I think they thought I was going to bring Josephine back. But she was already dead. *(He blinks back tears.)*

LYDIA. You saved this child. You enabled her to live.

ENOCH. Don't rhapsodize about it.

LYDIA. I think it's quite remarkable. A commendable thing.

ENOCH. I did what was required.

LYDIA. You've never delivered a baby before.

ENOCH. I've delivered hundreds of calves.

LYDIA. But people are not animals.

ENOCH. We all give birth and die. Just the same. *(He rises, looks in the match holder.)* We got any more matches?

LYDIA. In the cupboard. You already lit the lamp.

ENOCH. It's still dark in here.

(ALBERTINE enters, picks up a knife.)

ALBERTINE. Now I have to cut my hair.

LYDIA. Cut your hair for what?

ALBERTINE. For Josephine. *(ALBERTINE moves to the table.)* Wolf believed that when we die, it should last two days and then the dead come back to life. But Coyote said, "Oh no, when we die, it should last forever." And so it does.

LYDIA. Well yes, in a sense it does. But we believe you will see Josephine again. In the next life. And that she will be happy and beautiful just like you remember her—

ALBERTINE. Don't talk about her. She will only want to come back. And she cannot come back. She has to go on.

LYDIA. Whatever you say.

ALBERTINE. And then when Coyote's son Magpie died, Coyote wanted to change the rule. Make death last just two days instead of forever. But he couldn't. So he laid out on the ground looking up at the sky where crows were flying. And he grabbed a crow from the sky and pulled it to pieces he was so mad.

LYDIA. That's a beautiful story, Albertine. *(LYDIA slips the knife from ALBERTINE's hand.)*

ALBERTINE. Yes.

LYDIA. That's how you feel when someone dies.

ALBERTINE. Yes. *(ALBERTINE exits outdoors.)*

ENOCH. Where's the other coal oil lamp?

LYDIA. Over the sink, dear. "If it was a snake it woulda bit ya." *(ENOCH lights another lamp.)* Do you think we ought to take her?

ENOCH. Take who?

LYDIA. The baby.

ENOCH. No.

LYDIA. She's a beautiful child, Enoch. I want to give her a bath. She's still covered with blood.

ENOCH. No.

LYDIA. What's wrong with raising a little Indian child?

ENOCH. "A little Indian child." Good God, you sound like a bedtime story.

LYDIA. Curly hair, like Little Bone.

ENOCH. We're not taking that baby.

LYDIA. Why not? The Church wants them taken in.

ENOCH. Then let the Church take them in.

LYDIA. If she had the proper chance and were raised in the proper way, don't you think she could succeed?

ENOCH. Lydia, will you have done with this?

(ALBERTINE reenters with a bucket, fills it with water from the pitcher, and places it on the stove. Then exits.)

LYDIA. We've got to do something to help that woman.

ENOCH. She doesn't need our help. Doesn't want it.

LYDIA. Give me three good reasons why we shouldn't take the baby.

ENOCH. I don't want it, I don't want it, I don't want it.

LYDIA. What would it take for you to change your mind?

ENOCH *(exploding irrationally)*. You give 'em a house, they chop the floors out for firewood. You give them boots, they lose the laces. You drill them in English, they speak Shoshone the minute they walk away from you. Nothing would change my mind!

LYDIA. And yet you were fond of Josephine. You taught her in school.

ENOCH. I teach them all in school, Lydia.

LYDIA. But she had great promise. You said she did.

ENOCH. Her mother had promise. Carried a basket of rocks into salt flats, middle of summer, never returned.

LYDIA. Pauline was troubled. But Josephine...she was your favorite. She could amount to something, you said she could.

ENOCH. One of them comes along, one with promise, you send them off to boarding school.

LYDIA. We took her to the school in Brigham City. We drove her up there ourselves.

ENOCH. Cut her hair, deloused her. Gave her a uniform, assigned her a bed. Made her speak English, punished her for speaking Shoshone.

LYDIA. And she was a beautiful girl when she came back that next summer. Completely transformed.

ENOCH. What'd she do with it?

LYDIA. Got involved with some white man. Had that child, Little Bone. That was her fatal flaw, I suppose.

ENOCH. She never should have come back here.

LYDIA. But she worked for you. She did very well. She could have become a teacher, you said. If they'd let them.

ENOCH. Hung around with the worst of them, drunk the day the checks came in, starving in between.

LYDIA. You did your best.

ENOCH. Pretty damn pitiful best.

LYDIA. What about a cup of tea?

ENOCH. No thanks.

LYDIA. A little toast from breakfast?

ENOCH. No. *(Pause.)*

LYDIA. Enoch...

ENOCH. Yes.

LYDIA. Who's the father of this baby?

ENOCH. It doesn't matter.

LYDIA. Of course it matters.

ENOCH. How should I know?

LYDIA. You know. You know everything about her. *(Pause. ENOCH says nothing. Stares into the lamp.)* She's yours, isn't she? Josephine was the best student you ever had. They're both yours.

(Pause. ALBERTINE enters, picks up the bucket of water from the stove.)

ALBERTINE. I am going to the dance hall now.

ENOCH. To wash the body.

ALBERTINE. Yes.

ENOCH. I'll help you.

ALBERTINE. It is my job.

ENOCH. I know it is. But I can help you.

(ALBERTINE eyes him. She picks up the knife and cuts her ear. She rubs blood across her face. ENOCH takes the knife, cuts his ear, rubs the blood across his face.)

LYDIA. Enoch. What are you doing?

ALBERTINE. I will carry the water.

ENOCH. I can help you.

ALBERTINE. The load is light enough to float.

ENOCH. Light enough to float. If I help. *(He picks up the bucket.)* I'll follow you.

LYDIA. Where are you going?

ALBERTINE. To the dance hall. To wash the body and blood of Josephine.

LYDIA. Yes.

ALBERTINE. And later, home to care for Taipo Mea and
   Little Bone.
LYDIA. Of course.
ALBERTINE *(begins a mournful chant).*
   Bioh pahna
   Biah vina
   Biah vivi oh
   Hah nah.
LYDIA. Enoch, what's she doing? *(ENOCH joins in the
   chant. His eyes are fixed on ALBERTINE, and hers on
   him. Quietly:)* Enoch...
ALBERTINE & ENOCH.
   Bioh pahna
   Biah vina
   Biah vivi oh
   Hah nah.

*(After several seconds, LYDIA retreats upstage. She is
alone. The chanting continues. Lights dim.)*

INTERMISSION

Scene V: 1950s

*(The scene is the same. LYDIA's collection of porcelain
figurines has grown, and there are frames of Indian artifacts on the wall. A small Christmas tree is in the corner.
It is night. LYDIA enters, now middle-aged, and ever eager to make things right. She carries Christmas gifts.)*

LYDIA. It's a generation later, 1956. We're still in the
same house, Enoch and me. Emma's old place. Enoch's

not teaching anymore. He lost his zeal, so to speak. Well, several things happened to cause that. Anyway, he's trying to make a go of the farm instead. Albertine is gone. But Maud Moon and Bone, her great-great-grand-children, they've taken her place, you might say.

(MAUD MOON, enters and sits alone on the porch. She carries a wrapped Christmas gift.)

MAUD MOON *(singing).*
    Bioh pahna
    Biah vina
    Biah vivi oh
    Hah nah.
    (BONE joining her.)
    Biah vivi oh
    Hah nah.

(BONE enters and plops down on the step next to her. He wears an army jacket and a knit cap. He's had a few drinks and carries a can of beer, which he finishes and is about to throw offstage. MAUD MOON stops him. He puts the can back in his pocket.)

BONE. Hey you, baby sister.

MAUD MOON. Hey you, big brother.

BONE. Albertine, she singing to you?

MAUD MOON. 'Fraid so.

BONE. She don't want us to leave here, you know.

MAUD MOON. She don't want us to obey nobody's orders.

BONE. Because she never obeyed.

MAUD MOON. They told her to move to the Ute Reservation. She even signed something saying she'd go. And then she never went.

BONE. She left us, though, didn't she?

MAUD MOON. Not till we was raised.

BONE. Hey, I ain't raised, Maud Moon. Hell, I'll never be raised.

MAUD MOON. You been to the army, Bone. You been to Korea. You can do anything now. Who else on this porch has been to the army?

BONE *(starts to laugh).* You shoulda seen this, Maud Moon. You shoulda seen it. This guy, this other Half Blood, says he'd give me a quart of whiskey and the entry fee to the rodeo if I'd get on a bucking bronco.

MAUD MOON. What rodeo?

BONE. State Fairgrounds.

MAUD MOON. Oh God, Bone.

BONE. No, no, listen to me. I draw the last ride. Number eight. Everyone ahead of me is eating dirt. No one sticks their ride. Then it's my turn. And I've drawn this roan horse. Damn, if it ain't that colt I sold them guys in Payson that time. Remember him? He's a little older now, and I'm a little drunker. But we recognize each other. And we got an agreement. He's gonna rare up and kick. But he ain't gonna twist. And that's what he does. It looks good, but it's easy to stick. And I stick him, Maud Moon. Come away with eighty dollars and a quart of whiskey. What you think of that, Maud Moon? *(He laughs.)* Don't you think that's funny, Maud Moon? *(She looks at him. She's weary of this kind of story.)* Albertine was tough.

MAUD MOON. I know she was.

BONE. And I am tough.

MAUD MOON. I guess so.

BONE. She walked into that pond, middle of winter.

MAUD MOON. Yeah, she did that, Bone.

BONE. Because she hated that pond. And she was tough. Walked out on the ice and fell through. Couldn't get her out till spring. Now that is tough!

MAUD MOON. Wanted to poison Uncle Enoch's pond, that's what she really wanted.

BONE *(chuckling)*. 'Cuz she was tough.

MAUD MOON. Wonder what she'd do with the Termination Policy.

BONE. Terminate them! Terminate the whites! If they can tell us we ain't Indians no more, she could tell them they ain't whites no more. 'Cuz she was tough.

MAUD MOON. 'Cuz she was tough.

BONE. Yeah. *(Pause. They're looking at the sky.)*

MAUD MOON. You ready to go in?

BONE. Not me, Maud Moon. Let's just stay out here. *(Pause.)*

MAUD MOON. Looks like bullet holes in the sky.

BONE. Let's just stay out here forever.

MAUD MOON. Set up camp on Aunt Lydia's front porch.

BONE *(imitating LYDIA)*. "Oh she'd just love that, wouldn't she?" *(They laugh.)*

MAUD MOON *(moves to get up)*. Come on, let's go in.

BONE. No, I can't go in yet, Maud Moon.

MAUD MOON. Why not?

BONE. I gotta have a drink 'fore I go in there.

MAUD MOON. No you don't, Bone.

BONE. Promise I do.

MAUD MOON. You need to straighten up and act like a person.

BONE. I can do that, I can do that, Maud Moon. But I need just a little drop of Thunderbird.

MAUD MOON. Bone, please…

BONE. What they want with us, anyway?

MAUD MOON. What you think they want?

BONE. To know about Little Dougie.

MAUD MOON. That's a start.

BONE. "Why did you come home, you damn dumb Indian, and why didn't he come home, that smart white Mormon?"

MAUD MOON. It's also Christmas.

BONE. Oh, right. Christmas. I just love Christmas.

MAUD MOON. Sure you do.

BONE. All them used clothes we used to get at boarding school. I loved them. And all them new brooms and boxes of Tide we used to get from Aunt Lydia. I loved them—

MAUD MOON. That's enough, Bone. Here, hold this. *(She puts a wrapped gift in his hands.)*

BONE. What ya got here?

MAUD MOON. New plug-in coffeepot.

BONE. Ohhhh. You're so good, Maud Moon.

MAUD MOON. And you're so full of *qweecha*. *(They're laughing. MAUD MOON stands and readies to knock.)*

BONE. Wait a minute. Wait a damn minute.

MAUD MOON. What is it?

BONE. They know about this? *(Indicating his arm.)*

MAUD MOON. I don't know. I don't think so.

BONE. Then should I tell 'em?

MAUD MOON. Up to you, Bone.

BONE. My arm fell down on a knife. Both arms fell down on a knife. Oh-oh, accident of fate. *(They laugh again. MAUD MOON readies to knock.)* Wait a minute, wait a damn minute.

MAUD MOON. What is it now?

BONE. I'm scared of her, Maud Moon.

MAUD MOON. She was very good to us.

BONE. What if I can't remember all the words that start with "P"?

MAUD MOON. I can.

BONE. You always could.

MAUD MOON. Pitiful, poor, and poop!

(They're laughing again. BONE falls against the door just as LYDIA opens it.)

LYDIA. Well, Merry Christmas, Merry Christmas to you both.

BONE. Merry Christmas, Aunt Lydia. *(BONE hands her the package.)*

LYDIA. Why, thank you, Bone. And do come in. *(They follow her in.)* Could I get you something hot to drink?

BONE. Yeah, I'll have a hot...Budweiser.

LYDIA. Remember how you two used to sit up at this table, drinking hot Kool-Aid from coffee cups?

BONE. I'll have a cup of hot Virginia Dare.

MAUD MOON. Maybe you ought to open up your present.

LYDIA *(opens it enough to read the box)*. Don't tell me you got me a coffeepot.

MAUD MOON. I got tired of watching you make coffee in a pan.

LYDIA. Well, thank you, so much, but the church disapproves of coffee, you know.

BONE. We won't tell 'em, Aunt Lydia. We won't say a thing. *(He zips his lips and throws away the key. LYDIA giggles and sets the box down by the tree.)*

LYDIA. We got gifts right here for the two of you. A new set of towels for you, Maud Moon. For your new house. Your new life in the city.

MAUD MOON *(slight pause. Flatly)*. Thank you, Aunt Lydia.

LYDIA. And Bone, this is for you, *The Complete Works of William Shakespeare*. I want you to read *Hamlet*.

BONE. Right, Aunt Lydia.

LYDIA. It's about a young man who refuses to do what he must do. And other people die for it. *(Empty pause. They sit.)* Well, Merry Christmas, Merry Christmas to you both. *(Another awkward pause.)* My gracious, dinner! *(LYDIA picks up a plate containing a raw steak and moves it to the sideboard.)* Little Dougie was such a lover of Christmas, you know. Even after he grew up, he was a child again at Christmas. *(She sighs.)* Bikes and trains and little toy soldiers.

(ENOCH enters. He's wearing overalls. He spots BONE.)

ENOCH *(laughing)*. Jesus Christ, if it ain't you. Overwhelming success of the goddamn century!

BONE. Merry Christmas, Uncle Enoch.

ENOCH *(laughing)*. Good God, you screw up everything you touch. Ain't that the case?

BONE. Yeah. That's pretty much the case.

ENOCH. Can't even kill yourself right. Hell, if you was blowing a hole in your head, you'd miss. Ain't that the case?

LYDIA. That's enough, Enoch.

BONE. You got a drink, Uncle Enoch?

ENOCH. God almighty, you drive a truck into a cedar tree, and that cushions the blow. You saw up your arms with a knife that's too dull. Then you take a week's worth of Phenobarbital. And still you can't make it work. *(Laughing.)*

BONE. Look at it this way. I'm good for a laugh, ain't that right? *(A forced laugh, too loud, too long.)*

ENOCH. That's right. You're good for a laugh.

BONE. Arm fell on a knife. Both arms fell on a knife. *(Another forced laugh.)*

ENOCH. 'Course they did. Good God...

LYDIA. Enoch, hush now. Please.

ENOCH. Next time I hear you've attempted something, I want to hear about your success.

LYDIA. That is not funny, Enoch.

ENOCH. 'Course it is. Boy says it's funny, it's funny.

BONE. You got any whiskey hid in the bedroom, Uncle Enoch?

ENOCH. That what you learned in the army?

BONE. Yeah. I learned that in the army.

MAUD MOON *(pulls a frame from her bag)*. Look at this. Little Bone brought you both this picture of his outfit.

BONE. Don't show 'em that.

MAUD MOON. See there, Dougie's the commander.

BONE. Not the commander, the second lieutenant.

MAUD MOON. Ain't that the commander?

BONE. No it ain't the commander. It's the second lieutenant.

MAUD MOON. Anyway, he thought you could put it up on your wall.

BONE. Don't put that on the wall. Put a handful of hamburger and an empty helmet, you want to put something on the wall.

MAUD MOON. You don't need to be disgusting.

BONE. I'm telling the truth, Maud Moon!

(ENOCH moves to the sideboard, gets a hammer and nail.)

LYDIA. And how good to see you both. Maud Moon, looking more like her mother every day. Doesn't she, Enoch?

ENOCH. Doesn't she what?

LYDIA. Doesn't she look like her mother? *(ENOCH pounds the nail and hangs the photo.)* And doesn't Bone look fit? Of course, I remember him when he was just a tike. How good he was with numbers. As a child, he understood the concept of division. You can teach the children their tables, but they never understand the concept. But Bone understood. Most remarkable thing.

BONE. Comes natural, Aunt Lydia. If you're an Indian on the rez, you understand division.

LYDIA. And dear Maud Moon, she was always good at… well, at everything. Just like her mother, Josephine. And her mother was the best student Enoch ever had. We drove her to the Indian School in Brigham City ourselves, didn't we, Enoch? And she could have amounted to…

(ENOCH takes a bottle of whiskey from beneath the sideboard. He takes the bottle and two glasses to the table and pours two healthy drinks, hands one to BONE.)

ENOCH. Here you go. Drink that. Then tell me what you learned in Korea. *(BONE downs the glass. ENOCH indicates the bottle. BONE pours another drink.)*

MAUD MOON. Uncle Enoch, you don't give him booze and then ask him about that damned war.

ENOCH. This don't concern you, Maud Moon. This is between me and Bone. This is talk about war. And war ain't a pretty business.

BONE. What you know about war? You spent the last war teaching school. Sitting on your backside, talking too loud. "You start sheering a sheep from the head..." What you know about war?

ENOCH. I also farmed this land, Bone.

BONE. You couldn't farm this land. Spring dried up. That's why you was teaching school and having your way with my mother—

MAUD MOON. That's enough, Bone.

ENOCH. I want to know something, Bone. I want to know about Douglas. *(ENOCH hands him the bottle.)* The government says he may have froze to death. Is that right? Did he freeze to death?

LYDIA. Please don't ask these questions, Enoch. It doesn't matter. We don't need to know.

BONE *(a diversion)*. Remember that time I pantsed him?

LYDIA. Oh my goodness, yes.

BONE. He says I stunk up the schoolroom. So I pantsed him.

ENOCH. And for that, I tied you to that locust tree out there for five and a half hours. Give you time to think about it, didn't I, Bone?

BONE. Yep, you did, Uncle Enoch.

ENOCH. Then I made you clear the sagebrush from that potato field out there. Took you two whole days. Didn't it, Bone?

BONE. Yep, it did, Uncle Enoch.

ENOCH. And you didn't do nothing like that ever again, did you, Bone?

BONE. No, Uncle Enoch, I didn't.

ENOCH. Just like breaking a horse. Training a dog. Have to show 'em who's boss.

MAUD MOON. Bone is not a dog or a horse, Uncle Enoch.

ENOCH. Didn't say he was. Said the principle was the same. *(He shoves the bottle closer to BONE.)* I'm asking you a question, boy. What happened to Douglas?

MAUD MOON *(takes the bottle)*. Bone, look at me. I'm Coyote looking for my brother, Wolf. Wolf that created the world. Wolf that killed a thousand of the enemy with a single arrow. Wolf that defeated the tribe of the sister snakes. I'm Coyote. I cannot find my brother. All I got is his hide. Every morning I water the hide and check to see if he's come back. I want him back and all I got is his hide.

(BONE looks at her, takes the bottle back, takes a swig.)

ENOCH. Tell me what happened to Douglas. You know. You was there. *(BONE looks at ENOCH. Long pause.)* I'm listening.

BONE. You're listening, all right. First time in your life you ever listened.

ENOCH. What happened to him? You know. *(Another pause.)*

BONE *(lying)*. I don't know what happened to Little Dougie.

ENOCH. You do, goddamnit.

BONE. No, I don't, Uncle Enoch.

ENOCH. You tell me or there will be hell to pay.

BONE. Go ahead. Pay hell!

MAUD MOON. He don't know, Enoch. He says he don't know.

ENOCH. I'll never forgive you for this!

BONE. There's a few things I won't forgive you for neither!

LYDIA. You both served your country together. That's what I think is so remarkable.

BONE. I didn't serve my country, Aunt Lydia.

LYDIA. You most certainly did. And we are proud of you both for doing it. Aren't we, Enoch?

BONE. I didn't serve my country. I served my people.

MAUD MOON. He proved himself, Aunt Lydia. That ain't the same.

LYDIA. You were fighting for freedom. To keep those people free from Communism.

MAUD MOON. He was fighting to prove himself. The only way he could.

BONE. And don't ask me nothing else. Don't tie me to that tree, make me clear brush. You don't know what you're talking about. You never been in a damn war. It ain't like training a dog. Or breaking a horse. *(He breaks down. He looks at MAUD MOON.)* And I'm only the hide of Wolf. *(An uncomfortable pause.)*

LYDIA *(changing the subject)*. How nice to see you. Both of you. It's the children that make a Christmas. That's what I always say to Enoch. Oh, and I bet you're both excited about your new life. That's the nature of youth. A new life again and again. What an exciting time for both of you.

MAUD MOON. Termination Policy, it ain't exciting, Aunt Lydia. Telling us we ain't Indians, ain't Goshutes, ain't members of a tribe.

LYDIA. A new house, a new life. Oh, I think it's very exciting.

MAUD MOON. It's a government order to leave home, Aunt Lydia. Move to the damn city.

LYDIA. You're just a little nervous.

ENOCH. Best thing that could happen to you people. Get you off the government udder.

MAUD MOON. And give you another two hundred acres to farm.

LYDIA. Oh, I just know you'll both be very successful in your new life. Maud Moon a nurse. Little Bone, well, any number of things. *(BONE, staring at ENOCH, takes off his jacket, begins to unwrap the bandages on his arms.)* Each of you in a house, maybe an apartment in the middle of the bustling city. There will be things to do, places to go. Such excitement for you both. *(BONE grabs the bottle of whiskey, empties it. LYDIA is oblivious.)* You'll both have jobs and friends and there will be parties to go to, shopping to do. Activities of church and state. A whirlwind, a virtual whirlwind. *(BONE picks up a piece of meat from the top of the cupboard.)* We will visit sometime. But you'll have your jobs and your lives, your friends and your places to go and things to see. And so we won't stay long. *(BONE grabs a hammer and a nail.)* We'll just stay long enough to wish you well and satisfy ourselves that you have arrived. Happy young people with purpose and power.

(BONE nails the piece of meat to the wall, covering the photo.)

Scene VI: 1970s

(BONE enters.)

BONE. White people always said they'd make the desert
  bloom like a rose. Well, you oughta know what they got
  planted out here. Just a few miles south is Dugway
  Proving Grounds. They test chemical weapons and bio-
  logical weapons. Anything poison. At first, rats was
  showing up with growths on their heads, lizards without
  legs. Then a few years ago, they killed six thousand of
  our sheep, testing VX gas. Just a test. It worked. Over-
  head they fly missiles. See how accurate they are when
  they land. They ain't. Then little north of here is
  Envirocare. They store low-level nuclear waste. Yeah,
  it's blooming out here, all right. But it ain't like no
  damn rose.

  Anyway, it's a generation later, 1975. Lydia and Enoch
  still live in the old house. Twenty more years of accu-
  mulated stuff collecting around them. By the way, I ain't
  in this scene. I'm in jail. I kicked the booze, though.

  *(MAUD MOON, comes up to the outside door. She car-
  ries a large package. Sound of a doorbell.)*

  Oh, and my baby sister, Maud Moon, she's a political
  activist now.

  *(LYDIA hurries across the floor, dressed in a housecoat.
  She's old and frail.)*

LYDIA. Oh, my dear. You've come to pay a call. What a thoughtful girl you are. Always such a thoughtful girl.

MAUD MOON. I gotta talk to Enoch.

LYDIA. But of course. You've always had so much to say to one another.

MAUD MOON. Is he here?

LYDIA. Well, yes, naturally, he's here. *(Calling.)* Enoch. It's Maud Moon, come to pay a call. *(Back to MAUD MOON.)* And just look at you. You've let your hair…

MAUD MOON. Grow. Yes.

LYDIA. And you've got that… *(Indicating forehead.)*

MAUD MOON. Bandanna. Yes.

LYDIA. But then, I always liked your hair when it was short. You looked so smart. Like you could take on any job—

MAUD MOON. I just came to talk to the old man. It's kind of important.

LYDIA. Of course it is. *(Calling.)* Enoch! Maud Moon is here. *(Back to MAUD.)* And how are the children, dear?

MAUD MOON. Trouble. Whitaker's got a car.

LYDIA. Whitaker has a car. Little Whitaker. Has a car. My goodness. And Havis?

MAUD MOON. Nothing.

LYDIA. Still no word.

MAUD MOON. Blame the city. And the goddamn Termination Policy.

LYDIA. That has to be a mother's deepest well of agony. The disappearing child. When Little Dougie turned up missing in Korea… *(She tears up. Calling.)* Enoch! You have company, dear, Maud Moon. *(MAUD MOON looks at the artifacts on the wall. Removes one of the frames from the wall.)* Remember that cradleboard your great-grandmother Albertine made for me? Made it for a boy, said I'd have a boy, and so I did. *(MAUD MOON takes another frame, sets it near the other. LYDIA watches her. Calling.)* Enoch! *(Back to MAUD MOON.)* Lately he hasn't even been able to hunt for arrowheads. He's just not well enough. *(MAUD MOON takes yet another frame down.)* The ward elders from the church were out here for a blessing yesterday, but he would have none of it. Doctors say it's in the bones now.

MAUD MOON. I brought some white sage for him. From Wounded Knee. *(She gets a bundle of sage from her bag, hands it to LYDIA.)*

LYDIA. Because you were there?

MAUD MOON. Yes.

LYDIA. Enoch read all about that demonstration.

MAUD MOON. Not a demonstration, Lydia. An occupation. The largest military action in this country since the Civil War.

LYDIA. And you were there?

MAUD MOON. Yeah. I was there.

LYDIA. You could have been arrested, dear. Shot...or something worse.

MAUD MOON. I was arrested.

LYDIA. Arrested, you? Oh my goodness, I don't even know anyone who's been arrested. Except your brother, of course. And how is Little Bone?

MAUD MOON. Getting out in a month.

LYDIA. Well, good. That boy had such a gift with numbers. I remember that—

MAUD MOON. Look, I've got to talk to Enoch.

LYDIA *(calling)*. Enoch, dear! *(Back to MAUD MOON.)* Have you seen the new hospital going up? I said to

Enoch just the other day, "My goodness, our own Maud Moon will be working there before too long."

MAUD MOON. No, I don't think so. I'm going back to the rez.

LYDIA. The reservation?

MAUD MOON. Yes.

LYDIA. There are no jobs over there, dear.

MAUD MOON. I have a plan.

LYDIA. A plan. But of course you do.

MAUD MOON. Can I talk to Enoch?

LYDIA. Now you're not to become a lay-around. I won't let you be a lay-around. A...what's your name for it?

MAUD MOON. A Hang-Around-the-Fort.

LYDIA. I won't let you.

MAUD MOON. I'm going to hunt and farm. Raise squash and beans. Like they used to.

LYDIA. Like who used to?

MAUD MOON. Like our people used to.

LYDIA. But, dear, there's no water over there.

MAUD MOON. I'm gonna take the spring.

LYDIA. But that isn't yours. Is it?

MAUD MOON. Who does it belong to?

LYDIA. Well, it belongs to Enoch and the family.

MAUD MOON. Enoch and the family got it how?

LYDIA. There was no one out here then.

MAUD MOON. Yes, there was, Aunt Lydia.

LYDIA. Well, that's a matter of opinion, dear.

MAUD MOON. I am not an opinion, Lydia!

LYDIA *(taken aback)*. You've come by to see us. And goodness gracious, I look a mess. And the house is in an uproar. *(LYDIA picks up the frames. MAUD MOON takes them back.)*

MAUD MOON. It's all right. I just need to talk to you and Enoch.

(ENOCH enters on a cane.)

ENOCH. I've heard it all already. Heard everything you said. You run off to those damned Indian hippies in South Dakota, then you come back here and make demands.

MAUD MOON. Can't you even say hello first? You old coot! *(She hugs him.)*

ENOCH. You're after something. I know you. And you can't have it.

MAUD MOON. Still as mean as an old diamondback rattler.

ENOCH. Strike first, ask questions later. What do ya want?

MAUD MOON. To make a trade.

ENOCH. I ain't trading with an Indian. I'm too old. Too sick. You'd just take advantage of me.

MAUD MOON. I wanna move back to the rez.

ENOCH. Oh for God sake...

MAUD MOON. It's my turn to live there now.

ENOCH. Follow your mother into disaster. Or your grandmother into the salt flats, your great-grandmother into my pond. Suicide runs in your family.

LYDIA. Enoch, please—

MAUD MOON. Goshutes been over there for ten thousand years.

ENOCH. Yep. Eating grasshoppers and crickets.

MAUD MOON. That's where we crawled up out of the earth. That's where we're supposed to be.

ENOCH. Hell, Coyote dumped the jar of you people out there, as a joke.

MAUD MOON. We were out there in the beginning and we are still there now.

ENOCH. You were there because no one else would have this godforsaken place. Unforgiving desert. No one else with half a brain would have it.

MAUD MOON. Until you Mormons came along.

ENOCH. It took crazy Mormons to figure out how to make a living out here.

MAUD MOON. Goshutes belong here. You white people are transients.

ENOCH. You belong here all right! You, the snakes, the lizards and the sagebrush.

MAUD MOON. And the rice grass, the service berries, the pine nuts, and jackrabbits.

ENOCH. Goddamn Dust Eaters.

MAUD MOON. This place is out of balance, Enoch. You're trying to make it into England or Pennsylvania. This ain't either one of them. It's a desert.

ENOCH. Goddamn right it's a desert and you fight like a soldier every damn day of your life to make it something more.

MAUD MOON. You're not going to understand me, Enoch. But then, we never understood you either.

LYDIA. I would like to live in England or Pennsylvania. The grass grows right up to the roads—

MAUD MOON. Damn Termination Policy dumped us in the city, Uncle Enoch, middle of the slum, toilets overflowing, hog fencing for doors. That's where we're supposed to live. "Make your fortune, open a restaurant, start a business," they tell us. "You're free to do anything you want." In the meantime, you guys take over a little more of our land.

ENOCH. That's still the best thing that ever happened to the Indians, take 'em off the welfare rolls.

MAUD MOON. I've lost a boy to the city, a brother to the bottle, and half my land to you.

ENOCH. I paid for your education.

MAUD MOON. In exchange for what? Our land.

ENOCH. Look, you're a clever girl, you're smart. Your mother was smart.

LYDIA. Oh yes, Josephine was the finest student Enoch ever had.

ENOCH. She was a talented girl.

MAUD MOON. My grandmother too. She was a talented "girl."

ENOCH. Pauline. Yes.

MAUD MOON. And my great-grandmother. My great-grandmother was a talented "girl."

ENOCH. Albertine. Of course.

MAUD MOON. They spoke to me. All of them.

ENOCH. Oh for God sake.

MAUD MOON. They told me to move back.

ENOCH. In some peyote dream they told you that?

LYDIA. You had a vision, Maud Moon?

MAUD MOON. Something like that.

LYDIA. Visions from other than the General Authorities are most likely of the devil, dear. I'm sure you remember that.

ENOCH. You're a certified nurse. What do you know about farming and hunting?

MAUD MOON. I will learn what I can in the time I have left.

ENOCH. Storybook Indian bullshit!

LYDIA. Enoch, dear, if you don't curb your tongue, there are some of us who will just have to leave the room.

MAUD MOON. I lost one boy, already. And I'm close to losing another. My brother Bone's getting out of jail next month. I want to bring them all back here.

ENOCH. And all you want from me is what?

MAUD MOON. Nothing. I want to make a trade. *(She takes a cradleboard from beneath a cover.)*

ENOCH. What the hell's that?

MAUD MOON. It's my cradlebasket. Albertine made it. She told me to give it to you when I was finished with it. Said you'd understand why.

LYDIA. Oh, sweetheart, what a lovely gift.

MAUD MOON. Now you've got two. One for each of your Goshute children.

(ENOCH cannot speak. He rubs the laces on the cradleboard.)

LYDIA. One for Little Dougie, one for Maud Moon and Bone.

ENOCH *(choked up)*. What do you want?

MAUD MOON. I want to buy back the spring.

ENOCH. We are not discussing water.

MAUD MOON. I only want the water that used to go through the reservation. That's all. Take out your dam.

ENOCH. I'm raising cattle out there.

MAUD MOON. Raise fewer of them.

ENOCH. You can't run an operation without water.

MAUD MOON. You're doing nothing with that spring water. Except letting cows walk through it.

ENOCH. I'm raising a pasture, fifty-five acres of alfalfa and a hundred and forty head of beef cattle.

MAUD MOON. Make do with less. Eat squash and beans. We'll share with you.

LYDIA. I think it's quite a lovely plan. We could will our water to Maud Moon. That way she would be our heir.

ENOCH. The place is worthless without water.

LYDIA. Oh I like the idea, Enoch. Our own special heir.

ENOCH. What the hell happened to Douglas? Answer me that!

(MAUD MOON takes another frame from the wall.)

LYDIA. You know I've been thinking, wondering, where is your uniform, Maud Moon? I hardly recognize you without your brisk white uniform.

MAUD MOON. I'm taking back the *noa-pekka*.

ENOCH. I know what I'm doing with those things. I'm going to donate them to the university.

MAUD MOON. They belong to us.

ENOCH. Listen here, I picked up every damned one of them myself.

MAUD MOON. Would you like me to call the Bureau of Land Management?

ENOCH. Those sons a bitches.

MAUD MOON. What if we went into the local ward house, took the sacrament trays because, well, because no one was using them? And what if we put a bunch of sacrament cups in a frame and hung them on the wall?

ENOCH. Why the hell ain't you working?

LYDIA. That's what I say. Work will answer all your woes. *(Singing.)* "Come with me. Can't you see. Bye bye blackbird."

MAUD MOON. We're going back to our roots.

ENOCH. Your roots, Maud Moon, are sleeping in a brush hut eating vermin from each other's hair.

MAUD MOON. We may have eaten vermin. But you ate us.

ENOCH. We what?

MAUD MOON. You ate us. White men ate the Goshutes.

ENOCH. No white man would eat another human being.

MAUD MOON. Except that you considered us animals.

ENOCH. We are all animals.

MAUD MOON. Thank you. Yes. *"Suten tuku sukka suten taipo tainnappe u paikkattsi, un takkui tekkanu."*

ENOCH. Speak English, goddamnit.

MAUD MOON. "The white man simply killed the Indian and ate his meat."

ENOCH. Who told you that?

MAUD MOON. Lillie Pete.

ENOCH. A deranged old woman.

LYDIA. Hush, Enoch. She was a sweet old lady. She worked for us after Albertine died.

MAUD MOON. *"Suten tuku sukka suten taipo..."*

ENOCH. English—

MAUD MOON. Very well. *(With the voice of someone reading a children's story.)* "But there was a time, you know, when all the animals were people..."

LYDIA. Oh yes, that's my favorite story. Bear is chasing Deer, and so Deer says to Crane, "Make a bridge." And so Crane stretches out her neck and Deer walks over the bridge and into the mountain beyond the water.

MAUD MOON. That's a story about the end of a war.

LYDIA. Yes, yes, of course it is. And what a lovely thought.

ENOCH. The answer is no.

MAUD MOON. I know what the answer is.

ENOCH. Good.

MAUD MOON. But I don't care what the answer is. I'm taking the water. You have a choice. Release the water from the pond, or we'll pack your dam with dynamite. *(MAUD MOON moves to the door. Thinks a moment. Picks up two frames.)* I'll take the little grass doll. The one Albertine made for your father. And I'll take the gloves, the mourning gift she gave to him. You can have the arrowheads and the spear points. And now...goodbye, Enoch. *(MAUD MOON leaves.)*

Scene VII: 1990s

(It is dark, the house is empty, abandoned, except for a few boxes of assorted stuff. The place has been empty for several years. MAUD MOON, now in her 60s, enters with a flashlight.)

MAUD MOON. <u>A generation later, the late 1990s. The old house is empty. Uncle Enoch and Aunt Lydia, both gone.</u> *(She looks around for a moment. Then she moves to a box on the floor, kicks it, opens its flap, then picks up a frilly porcelain figurine.)* You tried to civilize the desert, Aunt Lydia, make white dancing ladies of us all. I think you failed. *(She puts the figurine down on the windowsill. She hears a singing noise.)* Sounds like crickets in here. Uncle Enoch's plumbing. It still leaks and the water's been off for years. *(She moves offstage to check. Then returns.)* Albertine hated your pipes, Uncle Enoch, your pond. We all hated it. The dam of the damned. *(She trains the light on a door jam.)* Hey, Bone, I'm taller than you. Half an inch. Lookit that. "You're nothing but a runt!"

(She rubs the marks. A beat. We hear the sound of an approaching truck, see a set of headlights. They stop in front of the house. MAUD MOON grabs the figurine, switches off her flashlight, and scoots into the shadows. BONE moves cautiously into the house. He's older. His hair is long, and he carries a flashlight.)

BONE. Hey. Who we got here, huh? *(Silence.)* I seen you from the road. You got a flashlight. I know you're in here. *(MAUD MOON emerges from the shadows.)* Well, well, well, well. Look at who it is.

MAUD MOON. Hey, Bone.

BONE. What you doing here, Maud Moon?

MAUD MOON. What you?

BONE. I'm keeping people out of here till they bulldoze this place. It's part of my job.

MAUD MOON. Some job.

BONE. At least it *is* a job.

MAUD MOON. Whose truck you driving, Bone?

BONE. Tribal vehicle.

MAUD MOON. It's a bribe, we all know that. You drive their truck, they own your soul.

BONE. So what you looking for, Maud Moon?

MAUD MOON. I ain't looking for nothing, Bone.

BONE. I wouldn't want you taking nothing that don't belong to you.

MAUD MOON. I ain't taking nothing.

BONE. So then, what's that you got in your hand?

MAUD MOON. A little figurine, used to sit on the dining room table. Don't you remember?

BONE. That don't belong to you, Maud Moon.

MAUD MOON. I know it don't belong to me.

BONE. Then why don't you put it down?

MAUD MOON. You suddenly got a whole lot of up-righteousness, ain't you, Bone?

BONE. You could use a little more of that yourself, Maud Moon. You take that little dancer, drive it over to Wendover, pawn it for five bucks to throw in a machine. That ain't right, Maud Moon. Aunt Lydia would disapprove.

MAUD MOON *(with exaggeration, puts the figurine down)*. Get off your high horse, Bone. You act like a white man in a big hat.

BONE. No, I ain't a white man with a hat. I'm an Indian that's famous. You seen to that. Get my name in the paper, get all them white people to send you money. Blame it on me. What's that? Suing your big brother. What's that anyway?

MAUD MOON. It's all I got left, Bone.

BONE. All you got left is to get me in the paper? Get me into court?

MAUD MOON. I don't know any other way to stop you.

BONE. You can't stop me, Maud Moon.

MAUD MOON. I want you to tell Albertine what you're up to. Forty thousand tons of high-level nuclear waste. And you're gonna store it here.

BONE. This desert is full of poison already.

MAUD MOON. Don't mean you have to add to it.

BONE. They are gonna put that stuff out there, one way or the other. Don't matter what you do. The only question is whether we get paid for it or whether we don't. You want our people to survive, Maud Moon. Or you want our people to disappear? Simple as that.

MAUD MOON. You don't sell your children. You don't shoot your mother.

BONE *(snapping back)*. Indians the only ones use the Mother Earth card? You notice that? White people got a whole deck of cards. We got one. One measly card. Mother Earth.

MAUD MOON. Don't use white people as an excuse for anything.

BONE. Why not?

MAUD MOON. Their job is different from ours.

BONE. Their job is to have dominion. Golly, wonder what ours is?

MAUD MOON. The whole thing is filthy.

BONE. So is poverty. Now I'm gonna have to ask you to leave here, Maud Moon. This place don't belong to you.

MAUD MOON. I know it don't belong to me.

BONE. Who's it belong to?

MAUD MOON. Belongs to that nephew of Aunt Lydia and Uncle Enoch.

BONE. Wrong. Belongs to everyone. It's gonna be a road. Road for everyone.

MAUD MOON. A road to your damned garden of deadly delights.

BONE. That's right. So what's you doing here?

MAUD MOON. I don't know. Saying goodbye, maybe.

BONE. Well, I don't want you in here, walking around in the dark, tripping on something, getting hurt, and suing me. I wouldn't want that.

MAUD MOON. Oh for God sake, Bone.

BONE. That nephew of Aunt Lydia and Uncle Enoch. He wouldn't want you walking around here in the dark, trip-

ping on something, and then suing him. He wouldn't
want that neither.

MAUD MOON. Don't act like an ass.

BONE. I can't trust you no more, Maud Moon.

MAUD MOON. Well, we're even there. 'Cuz I can't trust
you neither. That's always the way it is with us. Grow
up in the same house. Spend our whole lives together.
And we can't agree on anything now. Who did this to
us, huh? Who did it?

BONE. White people.

MAUD MOON. White people didn't do this.

BONE. Yes they did, Maud Moon. They taught us how to
hate each other. And we learned our lessons well. For
example, Maud Moon, you never carry through on what
you promise.

MAUD MOON. What's you talking about?

BONE. How come that pond of Uncle Enoch's is still out
there? You promised you'd take it out. It ain't out,
Maud Moon.

MAUD MOON. I took it out once. You know that. You
helped me. Then Uncle Enoch borrowed a bulldozer
from the State Road. Said he'd put the dam back exactly
as many times as I took it out. And every time it would
be bigger, thicker, higher, stronger.

BONE. That's how it is with the waste storage, Maud
Moon. Either we control it or we lose all control. Just
exactly the same.

MAUD MOON. Uncle Enoch was an old man, sick and
dying. Out on that damned Caterpillar in the middle of
the night. Aunt Lydia crying at him to come in, crying at
me for setting him off. I didn't have the heart to do it
again. This ain't the same thing, Bone.

BONE. I want you out of here, Maud Moon. Otherwise, I'm taking action.

MAUD MOON. A long time ago, when animals were people, the sun was too hot. It burned the seeds, the berries, it dried up the springs and the lakes. It set fire to the bushes and boiled the water. Coyote was mad. He decided to shoot the sun.

BONE. But he didn't hit the sun. His arrow burned up before it got there.

MAUD MOON. The point is, it's crazy to shoot at the sun.

BONE. The point is, you can't hurt the sun.

MAUD MOON. This land cured you, Bone.

BONE. Then why ain't it cured you, Maud Moon?

MAUD MOON. And arrogance is the biggest sin. This land ain't arrogant.

BONE. That's for sure.

MAUD MOON. We been out here for ten thousand years. The only people smart enough and patient enough to learn how to live out here.

BONE. It's right for us to store that stuff. The uranium came from Navajo land in the first place. And so it's right for us to store it now.

MAUD MOON. The Navajos died in them mines, Bone. How many of them got rich?

BONE. We will do the job right.

MAUD MOON. But what's the job? Breathe dust and die young?

BONE. You don't trust us. We're just "dumb Indians," we can't do the job.

MAUD MOON. Bone, you're shooting the sun.

BONE. We're doing this for all the people. All the earth.

MAUD MOON. Coyote had a jug full of people. He dumped some out by the river. Some by the lake. Some in the woods. Coyote had only a few people left; the ugly ones and the stupid ones were all that were left. He dumped them out here.

BONE. So they could be Goshutes.

MAUD MOON. It reminds us not to take ourselves too seriously. It prevents us from shooting the sun.

BONE. Does it prevent us from being unemployed? Drinking too much? Throwing our money at machines? *(MAUD MOON moves to one of the boxes, kneels down in front of it. She pulls up a pot full of shards and arrowheads.)* Stay away from that stuff, Maud Moon.

MAUD MOON. I'm putting these back where they belong.

BONE. Putting what back?

MAUD MOON. Arrowheads and pot shards. Uncle Enoch's collection. I'm planting a garden. Putting them back where they belong.

BONE. The road's going right through here, you know.

MAUD MOON. I know. But long after that road is gone, this garden will still be here. Just like us. We have been here since the beginning. And we'll be here till the end. When there are no more of us, there will be no more of them. *(She moves past him. Standing on the porch, she looks back at him.)* I have to fight you, Bone. I have to. It's what I'm supposed to do. *(He joins her on the porch.)*

BONE. You gotta understand one thing, Maud Moon. I'm doing the right thing for our people.

MAUD MOON. Water babies swallow the dead. That's why the lake smells the way it does. It's where we go to die. Where the water babies live.

BONE. You think you're gonna die soon, Maud Moon?

MAUD MOON. Maybe we all are.

BONE. We ain't gonna die. The stuff is safe.

MAUD MOON. I can hear the water babies singing. They sing for you. *(She begins to chant.)*

BONE. Look at how many times they tried to kill us, and we didn't die. We are here and we will remain here. Can we agree on that? *(Humming, MAUD MOON steps off the porch.)* Can we agree on that, Maud Moon?

MAUD MOON *(stops chanting)*. We are here and we will remain here. We can agree on that. *(She begins to chant again.)*

    Bioh pahna
    Biah vina
    Biah vivi oh
    Hah nah.

(BONE shrugs and joins her in the chant.)

    Bioh pahna
    Biah vina

(She nods at him and extends the pan of shards to him. He takes a handful. The sound of their chanting grows.)

    Bioh pahna
    Biah vina
    Biah vivi oh
    Hah nah!

(Both toss the shards into the air. Blackout. And silence.)

END

DIRECTOR'S NOTES

DIRECTOR'S NOTES

DIRECTOR'S NOTES

DIRECTOR'S NOTES

DIRECTOR'S NOTES

DIRECTOR'S NOTES